The U

Beginner's Guide to the 555 Timer

Build the Atari Punk Console and Other Breadboard Electronics Projects

Dedication

To my wife, Jenn, for all your love, support, and patience.

Disclaimer

Only power the circuits shown in this book with common household batteries.

Contents

Introduction

While there are many books about the 555 timer, I feel most have been either too in-depth for a beginner, or so lacking in descriptions of the circuits that a novice might have a hard time learning how the circuit works. Also, most 555 books only show a schematic view of a circuit, and some beginners may need a breadboard view to start understanding how to connect it.

The target reader for this book is an electronics hobbyist who may have a basic understanding of electrical current flow and components and also wants to start building their own circuits from simple schematics. While someone with no electronics experience can follow along (and may even learn some basic electrical concepts), this book is not meant to teach electronics from the ground up. There are hundreds of books, magazines and internet articles more appropriate for that.

A couple of great resources to start learning electronics are *Make: Electronics: Learning Through Discovery* by Charles Platt (tiny.cc/MakeElectronics), and *Getting Started in Electronics* by Forrest M. Mims III (tiny.cc/GettingStartedMims).

I used Fritzing (a free program from fritzing.org) to make the circuit and schematic diagrams in this book.

Videos, articles, and more information about the projects in this book are at my website, Bent-Tronics.com.

A full kit to complete all of the projects in this book is available from Jameco.com (part #2244666) here: tiny.cc/555kit

Thank you for your purchase of this book. I sincerely hope you find it useful. If you do, please leave a review on Amazon.com or other appropriate sites, and help spread the word!

-Jesse Rutherford

Chapter 1: Breadboard Basics

What is a solderless breadboard? As the name suggests, a solderless breadboard doesn't require any soldering to use. It allows you to make electrical connections between components quickly, experiment easily and even reuse parts for other projects. The name "breadboard" may have come from a time when early electronic experimenters fastened their electronic components on top of an actual breadboard (a wooden board on which bread is cut) to test out their circuits. Ronald J. Portugal patented the first solderless breadboard for electronics use in 1973, Patent #228,136.

Fig. 1-1 shows an example of a typical modern-day solderless breadboard. However, many other types and sizes look different than this and are connected differently too. Sometimes people refer to the breadboard pictured in Fig. 1-1 as a "400 Point Solderless Breadboard." This name refers to how many holes, usually called tie points or connection points, are on the breadboard. These tie points are how you will be connecting the components together to make a completed circuit. You make these connections by inserting the legs, or leads, of the components into the holes on the breadboard.

Fig. 1-1
400 Point Solderless Breadboard

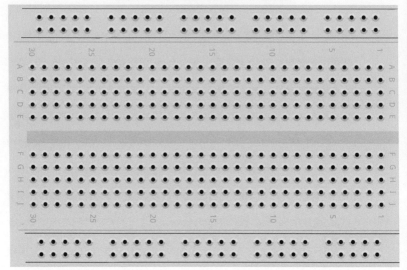

fritzing

The tie points are electrically connected internally in a particular manner depending on the size, make, and model of the breadboard. A typical 400 point breadboard is internally connected via terminal strips as represented by the different colored lines on the breadboard in Fig. 1-2. When in doubt, you can use a multimeter to check continuity between the various tie points to understand the configuration of a breadboard's terminal strips.

Fig. 1-2

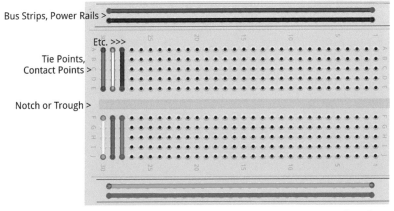

Bus Strips, Power Rails >

Etc. >>>

Tie Points,
Contact Points >

Notch or Trough >

fritzing

If a breadboard like the one pictured in Fig. 1-2 has one or two long terminal strips running the length of the breadboard along its edges; you can use these as power rails or bus strips. The horizontal lines in Fig. 1-2 designates these. Using these as power rails makes it easy to distribute positive (or negative) voltages and ground to multiple connections throughout your circuit. Fig. 1-3 shows how to connect a 9-volt battery's positive and negative posts to the "upper" power rails. One way to establish connections to various tie points on a breadboard is to use jumper wires made from #22 AWG solid-core hook-up wire. Other gauge wire from about #20 - #28 AWG will work, however, stranded hook-up wire doesn't work well at all for this. You can also purchase pre-formed jumpers in kits of predetermined lengths and colors.

Fig. 1-3

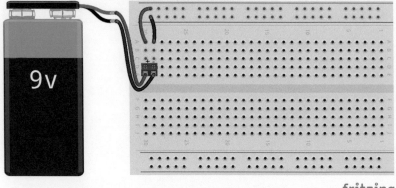

The shorter terminal strips that run perpendicular to the power rails are the main working area of the breadboard. In Fig. 1-2 these are represented by the vertical lines. A notch, or trough, runs down the middle of the breadboard. This trough (sometimes called a trench) makes it convenient to place an IC's (integrated circuit, a.k.a., chip) pins into the breadboard while keeping them electrically isolated from each other. The trough also allows you to place components closer to each other by using the "upper" and "lower" sections simultaneously while also remaining electrically isolated. Fig. 1-4 shows how a switch to turn power on and off to the breadboard can be added using the "upper" portion of the breadboard's terminal strips, and distribute the "upper" positive and negative power rails to the "lower" ones.

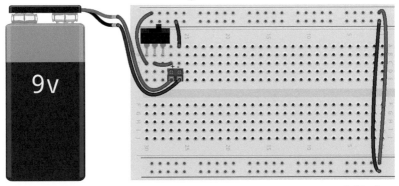

Fig. 1-4

fritzing

Now that you have a basic understanding of how a breadboard is connected take a look at a very simple schematic diagram of a basic circuit shown in Fig. 1-5. For some beginner electronics hobbyists, even this schematic can be hard to understand. To help you understand the relationship between the two, you will see the projects in this book presented as both schematic diagrams, and circuits configured on a breadboard. *Notice, as in Fig. 1-5, all ground symbols in each schematic connect to each other in real life.*

Then look at the same circuit as Fig. 1-5 set up on a breadboard in Fig. 1-6.

The "real world" view of components connected on a breadboard looks very different than the schematic diagram. To throw a little bit more confusion into the situation, no "correct" way to connect components together on a breadboard exists. Fig. 1-7 shows the same electrical current flow as Fig. 1-6, without using jumper wires.

Fig. 1-5
Example Schematic 1

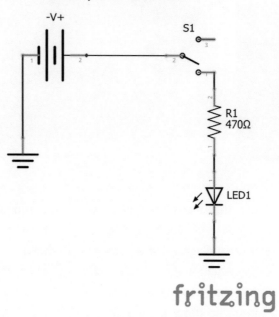

Fig. 1-6

Breadboard Layout of Example Schematic 1

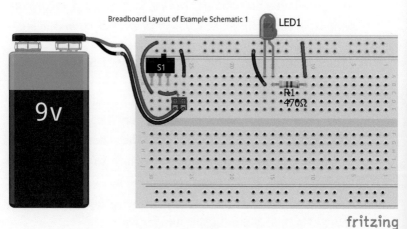

If you are new to electronics, it's a good idea to practice placing parts on a breadboard in the configurations shown in both Fig. 1-6 and Fig. 1-7. The sliding switch (S1) should turn the LED on and off. It will help to compare your breadboarded circuit to the schematic in Fig. 1-5 until you understand the relationship between them.

Note: an LED's anode (positive) leg is usually either longer than the other or has a bend in it or both. A flat spot on the LED's lens commonly designates the cathode (negative) side.

You could go on almost endlessly, finding various ways to connect components on the breadboard that still result in the same working circuit.

Fig. 1-7

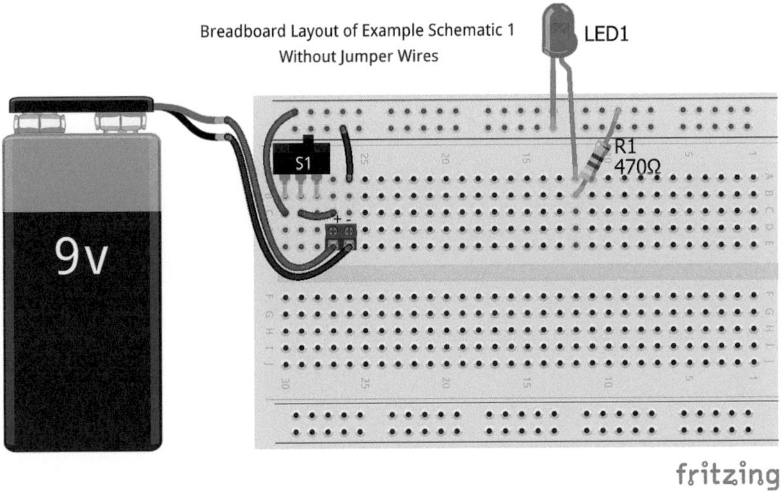

Breadboard Layout of Example Schematic 1
Without Jumper Wires

LED1

R1
470Ω

S1

9v

fritzing

•While every effort will be made for the projects in this book to have an easy visual layout and connections of components on the breadboard, know that there are many ways to accomplish the same results. Also, your parts and the ones in the illustrations may differ in size, shape, and color. Don't be afraid to customize the layout of your components in ways that may be more convenient or make more sense to you!•

Chapter 2: The Fantastic 555

The 555 timer was invented in 1971 by Hans R. Camenzind, and released in 1972 by the Signetics Corporation. They chose not to patent the design, and since then many manufacturers have made a version of this chip. In fact, the 555 timer may be the best selling IC of all time (over 1 billion a year for many years). While the 555's primary function is either a "one-shot" timer (monostable mode) or as an oscillator (astable mode), creative circuit design can lead to many other uses. There is also a dual version of the 555 timer called the 556, which is just two 555s in the same IC package, and even a 558 quad version of the 555 although it is slightly more limited than four actual 555 timers. There are other specialized versions of the 555 chip. However, this book will not cover those.

> •Interestingly, the 555 "timer" isn't in itself a timer at all. Its internal circuitry measures and compares the different voltages on its pins, which are dependent on the external components hooked up to it. It then outputs a voltage pulse (or series of pulses), of which the length (or frequency) depends on the values of these external components, and how they are connected.•

The circuits in this book will use a "standard" 555 timer chip. The markings on the outside will depend on the manufacturer, but will usually be along the lines of NE555, LM555 or similar. Be sure to find the data sheets that match the markings on your chip, so you know its specifications. While the 555 comes in a few different packages, the 8-pin DIP (Dual In-line Package) is used in this book.

Fig. 2-1 shows a representation of the 555 chip with the pins labeled. Fig. 2-2 illustrates the schematic view of the 555.

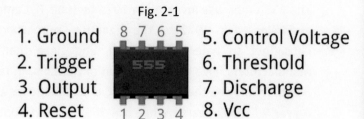

Fig. 2-1

1. Ground
2. Trigger
3. Output
4. Reset

5. Control Voltage
6. Threshold
7. Discharge
8. Vcc

fritzing

Fig. 2-2

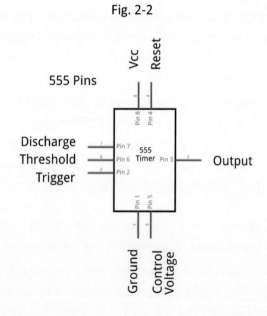

fritzing

555 Pin Functions:

Pin 1: *Ground-* This pin connects to ground (in this book, the negative terminal of a battery).

Pin 2: *Trigger-* The internal circuitry of the 555 monitors the voltage at this pin. When this voltage goes LOW (below 1/3 Vcc), the timing cycle of the 555 starts. In monostable mode, it may be necessary to keep this pin HIGH (connected to the positive supply voltage through a pull-up resistor) while waiting for the LOW trigger.

Pin 3: *Output-* This pin typically outputs a HIGH (close to the power supply voltage) pulse when on and LOW (close to 0 V) pulse when off. Depending on the specs and supply voltage of the particular 555, this pin can source (output) and sink (take in) up to 200 mA.

Pin 4: *Reset-* This pin will reset (or stop) the timing cycle when a LOW pulse is received. It is best to keep this pin HIGH (connected to the positive side of the power supply) when not in use.

Pin 5: *Control Voltage-* This pin allows an external control voltage to vary the timing of the 555, independently of the normal timing components. It is best to bypass this pin by connecting it to ground through a small (around .01 μF) capacitor when not in use.

Pin 6: *Threshold-* The internal circuitry of the 555 monitors the voltage at this pin. When this voltage goes HIGH (above 2/3 Vcc), the timing cycle ends.

Pin 7: *Discharge-* This pin discharges the timing capacitor.

Pin 8: *Vcc-* This pin connects to the positive side of the power supply voltage. +4.5 V to +16 V DC is typical. Check the data sheet for your particular model of 555 to be sure.

As mentioned before, the 555 has two main operating modes; astable, and monostable. Because the pins are connected differently in each of the two modes, the following chapters will explain more of the pin functionality.

Chapter 3: Basic Astable Mode

While most books on the 555 start with the monostable (one-shot) mode, this one will start with astable (oscillator, or multivibrator) mode. Why? Because soon you'll have a circuit put together that blinks a light, and then another that makes some noise. Who doesn't like flashing lights and sounds?

First, take a look at Fig. 3-1 which is a schematic diagram of a 555 circuit in the astable mode that flashes an LED. While using the 555 in the astable mode, there are only three components that have a direct effect on the timing cycle; R1, R2, and C1. You'll see them on the left side of the schematic. Other components can be added to manipulate the timing cycle further.

What's going on here? It will be easier to describe this circuit once you have it built on your breadboard and you can *see* what it's doing. Start by gathering the parts you'll need.

Fig. 3-1

Basic Astable Mode

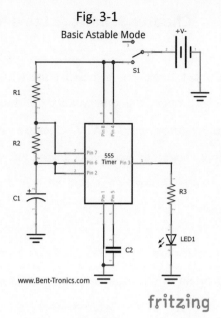

www.Bent-Tronics.com

fritzing

Fig. 3-2

Basic Astable Mode

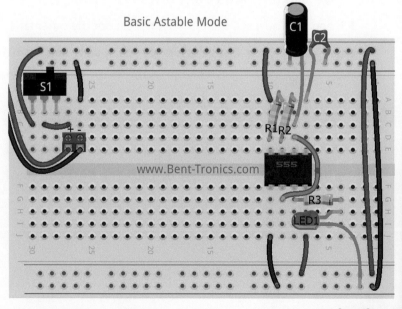

www.Bent-Tronics.com

fritzing

Project 1:

Parts List:

- Breadboard
- DC Power Supply (a 9-volt battery with some snap-on lead wires attached will do)
- Screw terminal block (one of many methods to hook your battery lead wires to the breadboard)
- Assortment of #22 AWG solid-core hook-up wires
- 555 timer
- S1 = Small SPDT slide switch
- **R1 = 1M Ohm*** (Brown, Black, Green)
- **R2 = 1M Ohm*** (Brown, Black, Green)
- R3 = 470 Ohm (Yellow, Violet, Brown)(or equivalent current limiting resistor for the LED)
- **C1 = 1 µF***
- C2 = .01 µF (optional, but recommended)
- LED1 = any common LED should work

- additional components for variations of this project as described below: two 1k resistors (Brown, Black, Red), one 47k resistor (Yellow, Violet, Orange), one each of 4.7 µF and .22 µF capacitors, and a small speaker

experimenting with these values will change the frequency/timing of the 555 - always switch the power off to the circuit before changing parts

First connect all of the parts, except the battery, on the breadboard as shown in Fig. 3-2.

Some helpful tips:

- Your parts may look different, or physically be a different size than Fig. 3-2, which may mean a slightly different layout on your breadboard.
- Be sure to observe the polarity markings on your parts. Make sure all anodes (positive) go towards the most positive side of the circuit, and all cathodes (negative) towards the most negative (ground) side of the circuit.
- If any parts seem like they won't fit, leave them off the breadboard and connect them with extra pieces of hook-up wire, which may require soldering.
- Double check, even triple check that all of your connections are correct, and that any wires or legs of any components aren't touching other components or wires.

Once you are confident that your connections are correct, make sure S1 is in its "off" position, then connect the battery, making sure to observe the polarity is correct. Now it's time for the "smoke test!" Slide S1 to the "on" position. What happens?

If everything is correct, you should see LED1 blinking on for about 1.3 seconds, and off for about .7 seconds. If so, congratulations! If not, slide S1 to the "off" position, disconnect the battery and re-check that all of your connections are correct and that the parts are the right values. Then try again.

•Here is a brief and simplified explanation of how this circuit works. Current flows to C1 through R1 and R2. The amount of time C1 takes to charge up to 2/3 Vcc is both affected by the overall resistance of R1 and R2, and the size of C1, which determines the length of the on portion of the cycle. Once pin 6 senses that C1 has charged to 2/3 Vcc; then C1 starts to discharge through R2 via pin 7, which determines the length of the off portion of the cycle. Since the off time is only affected by the size of C1 and R2, it will always be shorter than the on time (without other modifications to the circuit). Because a LOW voltage on pin 2 always starts the timing cycle, and since pin 2 connects to pin 6, when C1 discharges to 1/3 Vcc (LOW) it triggers pin 2, then the timing cycle starts over. Also, each time the circuit is powered up, the time C1 takes to charge is slightly longer than the rest of the cycles because it is charging from 0 volts instead of 1/3 Vcc. Fig. 3-3 displays a graphical representation of this oscillating charge/discharge process.•

Before continuing, here's the definition of some terms, and some equations for the astable mode.

Definitions:

Frequency- the rate of timing cycles per second, measured in Hertz (Hz)

Period- the length of one complete timing cycle, measured in seconds

On time- how long the timing cycle is HIGH

Off time- how long the timing cycle is LOW

Duty cycle- the ratio of on time, to off time, of one timing cycle, given in percentage

Equations:

Frequency: $f = 1.443/(R1+2*R2)*C1$

Period: $T = 0.693*(R1+2*R2)*C1$ or $T = t_1+t_2$

On time: $t_1 = 0.693*(R1+R2)*C1$

Off time: $t_2 = 0.693*R2*C1$

Duty cycle: $D = 100*(\text{on time})/(\text{on time} + \text{off time})$ or

$D = 100*t_1/(t_1+t_2)$

Note: R is in M Ohms, C is in μF, frequency is in Hz, Time is in seconds, Duty cycle is in %

Now for some math. Project 1 mentions that R1, R2, and C1 determine the on and off times of LED1 and some rough estimates of the times and frequency that it was blinking. Using the equations above, calculate what these times should be, using the components listed in Project 1, simplifying step by step.

$$f = 1.443/(R1+2*R2)*C1$$
$$f = 1.443/(1+2*1)*1$$
$$f = 1.443/(1+2)*1$$
$$f = 1.443/3*1$$
$$f = 1.443/3$$
$$\mathbf{f = .481\ Hz}$$

$$T = 0.693*(R1+2*R2)*C1$$
$$T = 0.693*(1+2*1)*1$$
$$T = 0.693*(1+2)*1$$
$$T = 0.693*3*1$$
$$T = 0.693*3$$
T = 2.079 seconds

$$t_1 = 0.693*(R1+R2)*C1$$
$$t_1 = 0.693*(1+1)*1$$
$$t_1 = 0.693*(2)*1$$
$$t_1 = 0.693*2$$
t_1 = 1.386 seconds

$$t_2 = 0.693*R2*C1$$
$$t_2 = 0.693*1*1$$
$$t_2 = 0.693*1$$
t_2 = 0.693

$$D = 100*t_1/(t_1+t_2)$$
$$D = 100*1.386/(1.386+.693)$$
$$D = 100*1.386/2.079$$
$$D = 100*.666$$
D = 66.6%

Whew! OK, so what does all of that mean? In theory, LED1 was blinking at a rate of .481 Hz. It was on for 1.386 seconds and off for .693 seconds. That means it took 2.079 seconds to complete one timing cycle (LED1 starts to blink every 2.079 seconds), and its duty cycle was 66.6%.

These times are in an ideal world with ideal components.

Take a look at the actual times and values on an oscilloscope (Fig. 3-3) to see what, if any, differences there were from your calculations.

Fig. 3-3

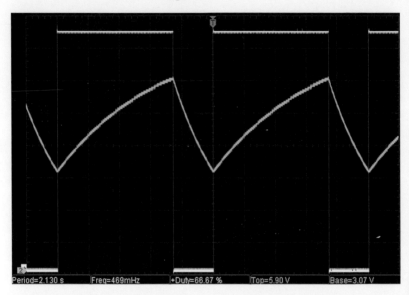

Period=2.130 s   Freq=469mHz   +Duty=66.67 %   Top=5.90 V   Base=3.07 V

The yellow square wave in Fig. 3-3 corresponds to the output (on and off time of the LED) of your circuit. According to the scope, the actual frequency was .469 Hz. The on time was 1.42 seconds. The off time was .71 seconds. The period of the total cycle was 2.130 seconds. The duty cycle was 66.67%. Those are *very* close to the calculated times!

•The blue wave on the scope in Fig. 3-3 (the one that looks like a shark's fin) shows C1 charging up during the on portion of the cycle until it reaches 2/3 (6 volts) of Vcc (9 volts), and discharging during the off portion until it reaches 1/3 (3 volts) of Vcc. Then the cycle starts over. As you can see, the actual voltages for 2/3 Vcc and 1/3 Vcc, in this case, are 5.9 V, and 3.07 V, respectively.•

Your times may differ slightly from the calculations and these actual results. That is due mainly to variation in the tolerances of the components, and a few other factors. Using components with lower tolerance values should lead to more accurate results. Now, time to start experimenting with some other values.

Project 1a:

Switch off S1, change out R1 to 1k Ohm, and R2 to 47k Ohm. Switch on S1. What changes, if any, do you see? You should see LED1 blinking at a much faster rate than before. It should be at about 15 Hz (very rapidly). That is because the resistor values are now smaller, and the time it takes to charge and discharge the capacitor, as a result, is quicker. Use the equations from above to calculate what the results should now be.

Project 1b:

Repeat this process. However, this time only change out R2 to 1k Ohm. After switching on S1, what do you notice? LED1 should appear to be on constantly. However, it is blinking so fast your eyes can't see it turning on and off. To verify this, change out LED1 with a small speaker. You should hear a tone of about 481 Hz. (R3 is optional. The only difference is the volume. A 10 µF capacitor in series before the speaker to block any DC is recommended for anything more than experimenting.)

Project 1c:

Until this point, you have only changed out the resistors to affect the timing cycles of your circuit. Now, repeat the process above, only leave the resistors and speaker in place, and only change out C1 to 4.7 µF. You should hear a lower pitched tone (around 102 Hz). The larger the capacitance of C1, the longer it takes to charge, and therefore is slower than having the 1 µF capacitor in place. What do you think happens if you change out C1 to a smaller capacitance? Try changing C1 to .22 µF. Did the pitch of the tone go up or down? What is its frequency? *Remember your equations.*

Feel free to experiment with the values of R1, R2, and C1; and whether you have an LED or speaker for the output. *Tip: Variable resistors for R1 or R2 (or both) like rotary potentiometers, CdS cells (a.k.a. photoresistors or LDRs) and a speaker for the output make for some interesting noise making. More of that in Chapter 7!* Also, you're not just limited to making a sound or blinking an LED. You can use this circuit for anything that needs to cycle on and off at a particular frequency. However, to switch bigger loads on and off, transistors, relays or other combinations of components will need to be used at the output. Fig. 3-4 is a graph that shows the relationship between the timing components and can help with selecting parts or calculating frequency. Also, there are many 555 timer calculators available for free on the internet.

•Here are some tips for selecting components for this circuit. C1 is usually the first one to select because there are usually fewer options for capacitor sizes. C1 can be any type capacitor, but the larger electrolytic types tend to be "leaky" and give less accurate results. Ceramic disc capacitors can be less accurate too. Tantalum, or Mylar and other film type capacitors usually work well. A low voltage rating for C1 in this circuit is fine, and may even work better than a higher voltage rating. Use whatever you have available for C1 for general experimenting, but use lower tolerance values and higher quality capacitors for projects that require greater accuracy, and the same goes for R1 and R2.

R1 should be about 1k Ohm minimum for best results. The total resistance of the equation in Fig. 3-4 of R1 and R2 doesn't have much of a maximum, but 10M Ohms is usually a practical upper limit. When R1 is smaller compared to R2, the duty cycle reaches closer to 50%. When R1 is larger compared to R2 in size, the duty cycle approaches 100%. •

Fig. 3-4

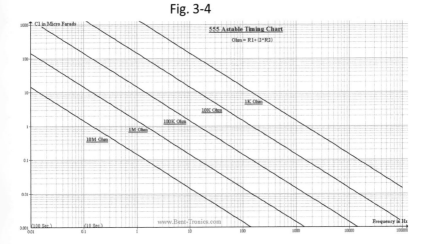

Chapter 4: Basic Monostable Mode

Now that you've got your fix of blinking and beeping in Chapter 3, you'll now learn how to set the 555 to turn on once for a predetermined amount of time in monostable (one-shot) mode. Because there's only an on period, rather than on and off periods like in astable mode, the monostable mode only requires one timing resistor, rather than two. You can see the difference between the two in the schematics in Fig. 4-1.

Fig. 4-1

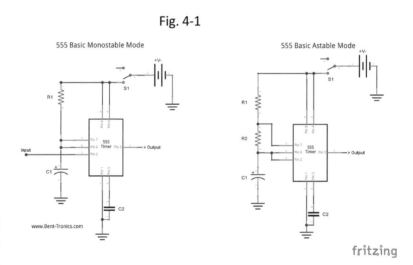

As Fig. 4-1 shows, the monostable version of the circuit doesn't have a timing resistor between pins 6 and 7. The version of the monostable circuit you will build next will also include a reset switch to stop the timing cycle and ready it to start again. Fig. 4-2 shows the schematic of this circuit.

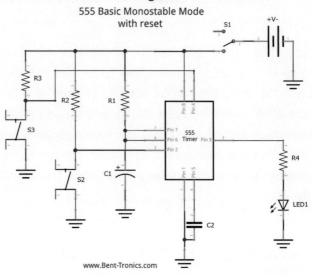

Fig. 4-2

555 Basic Monostable Mode
with reset

www.Bent-Tronics.com

fritzing

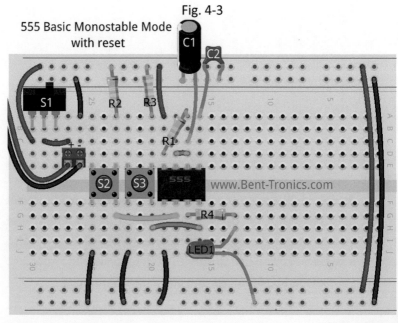

Fig. 4-3

555 Basic Monostable Mode
with reset

www.Bent-Tronics.com

fritzing

As in Chapter 3, it will be easier to explain this circuit once you have it built on your breadboard and you can *see* what it's doing. Time to get your parts in order.

Project 2:

Parts List:

- Breadboard
- DC Power Supply (a 9-volt battery with some snap-on lead wires attached will do)
- Screw terminal block (one of many methods to hook your battery lead wires to the breadboard)
- Assortment of #22 AWG solid-core hook-up wires
- 555 timer
- S1 = Small SPDT slide switch
- S2, S3 = Small SPST push button tactile switch
- **R1 = 1M Ohm*** (Brown, Black, Green)
- R2, R3 = 10k Ohm (Brown, Black, Orange)(pull-up resistors)
- R4 = 470 Ohm (Yellow, Violet, Brown) (or equivalent current limiting resistor for the LED)
- **C1 = 4.7 µF***
- C2 = .01 µF (optional, but recommended)
- LED1 = any common LED should work

- additional components for variations of this project as described below: one 150k resistor (Brown, Green Yellow), one each of 10 µF and .22 µF capacitors

experimenting with these values will change the timing of the 555 - always switch the power off to the circuit before changing parts

   Connect all of the parts except the battery on the breadboard as shown in Fig. 4-3.

Some helpful tips:

- For Project 2, connect the circuit on the "left" side of the breadboard as shown in Fig. 4-3, leaving room on the "right" side for Project 3 in the next chapter.
- Your parts may look different, or physically be a different size than Fig. 4-3, which may mean a slightly different layout on your breadboard.
- Be sure to observe the polarity markings on your parts. Make sure all anodes (positive) go towards the most positive side of the circuit, and all cathodes (negative) towards the most negative (ground) side of the circuit.
- If any parts seem like they won't fit, leave them off the breadboard and connect them with extra pieces of hook-up wire, which may require soldering.
- Double check, even triple check that all of your connections are correct, and that any wires or legs of any components aren't touching other components or wires.

Once you are confident that your connections are correct, make sure S1 is in its "off" position, then connect the battery, making sure to observe the polarity is correct. Slide S1 to the "on" position, and press S2. What happens?

If everything is correct, you should see LED1 turn on for about 5 seconds, and then turn off. Also, pressing S3 after S2 but before 5 seconds is up, should turn LED1 off.

If so, congratulations! If not, switch S1 to the "off" position, disconnect the battery and re-check that all of your connections are correct and that the parts are the right values. Then try again.

•Here is a brief and simplified explanation of how this circuit works. When pressing S2, pin 2 goes LOW triggering the start of the timing cycle and current starts to flow to C1 through R1. The amount of time C1 takes to charge up to 2/3 Vcc is both affected by the overall resistance of R1, and the size of C1, which determines the length of the on (HIGH) portion of the cycle. Once pin 6 senses that C1 has charged to 2/3 Vcc, then C1 will almost immediately discharge via pin 7, the output turns off (LOW), and the cycle is over. Also, pressing the reset switch (S3) brings pin 4 LOW and forces the timing cycle off (LOW). Fig. 4-4 displays this charge/discharge process.•

Different than astable mode, monostable mode only has one state to define, and therefore only one equation.

Definition:

Period- (T) the length of one complete timing cycle, measured in seconds

Equation:

Period: T = 1.1*R1*C1

Note: R is in M Ohms, C is in µF, Time is in seconds

Now for a little math. Project 2 mentions that R1 and C1 determine the on time of LED1 and a rough estimate of that time. Using the equation above, calculate what this time should be using the components listed in Project 2, simplifying step by step.

$$T = 1.1*R1*C1$$
$$T = 1.1*1*4.7$$
$$T = 1.1*4.7$$
$$T = 5.17$$

T = 5.17 seconds

OK, so that wasn't near as bad as the equations in astable mode, right? What does all of that mean? In theory, LED1 was on for 5.17 seconds. This time is in an ideal world with ideal components.

Now take a look at the actual time on an oscilloscope in Fig. 4-4 to see what, if any, difference there was from our calculation.

Fig. 4-4

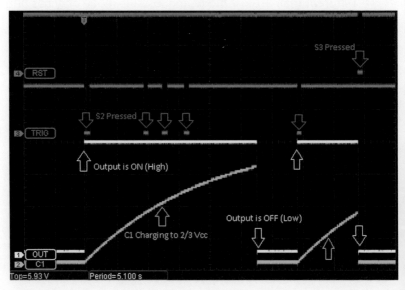

5.1 seconds actual, vs. 5.17 seconds calculated - that's pretty close!

> •So what does all of that other stuff on the oscilloscope display mean? Trace 3 (labeled TRIG) shows even if S2 is pressed multiple times during the timing cycle, nothing happens. Trace 1 (labeled OUT) shows the output (pin 3) is on (HIGH) for 5.1 seconds. Trace 2 (labeled C1) shows C1 charging up to 2/3 (6 volts) of Vcc (9 volts), which triggers the timing cycle to stop. The actual voltage of 2/3 Vcc was 5.93 V. Trace 4 (labeled RST) shows pressing S3 (reset) forces the timing cycle to stop, and the output turns off (LOW). •

Your time may differ slightly from the calculation and this actual result. That is due mainly to variation in the tolerances of the components, and a few other factors. Using components with lower tolerance values should lead to more accurate results. Now, time to start experimenting with some other values.

Project 2a:

Switch off S1, change out R1 to 150k Ohm. Switch on S1, and press S2. What changes, if any, do you see? You should see LED1 turn on for a shorter time than before. It should be about 1 second. That is because the resistor value is now smaller, and the time it takes to charge the capacitor, as a result, is quicker. Use the equation from above to calculate what the results should now be.

Project 2b:

Repeat this process. Change R1 back to 1M Ohm and change out C1 to 10 µF. Pressing S2 should turn LED1 on for a longer period than in Project 2. The larger the capacitance of C1, the longer it takes to charge, and therefore is slower than having the 4.7 µF capacitor in place. What do you think happens if you change out C1 to a smaller capacitance? Try changing C1 to .22 µF. Did LED1 stay on longer or shorter? What is its duration? *Remember your equation.*

Feel free to experiment with the values of R1, and C1. *Tip: A variable resistor for R1, like a rotary potentiometer, will vary the length of the timing cycle.* You can use this circuit for anything that needs to turn on for a predetermined amount of time and then turn off, including a pulse to trigger another circuit or device. However, to switch bigger loads on and off, transistors, relays or other combinations of components will need to be used at the output. Fig. 4-5 is a graph that shows the relationship between the timing components and can help with selecting parts or calculating times. Also, there are many 555 timer calculators available for free on the internet.

Fig. 4-5

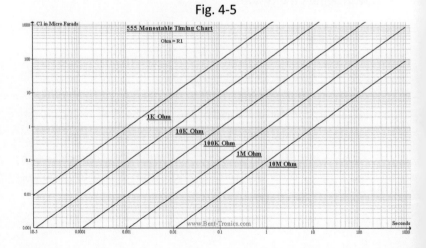

Chapter 5: Mixing Modes

There are many ways to combine both astable and monostable modes into one project. The schematic in Fig. 5-1 shows how the two circuits in Fig. 4-1 would look like connected so that the monostable 555 controls the length of time the astable 555 is flashing its LED.

As in the previous chapters, it will be easier to explain this circuit once you have it built on your breadboard.

•Here is a brief and simplified explanation of how this circuit works. The astable (Chapter 3), and monostable (Chapter 4) 555s work as described in their respective sections. The central concept to understand in this project is when the monostable 555's output pin is LOW it is keeping the reset pin of the astable 555 LOW. Pressing S2 switches the output of the monostable 555 to HIGH turning on its LED, enabling the astable 555 to run (its reset pin goes HIGH) until the timing cycle of the monostable 555 is over. Then both 555s return to their original states.•

Fig. 5-1

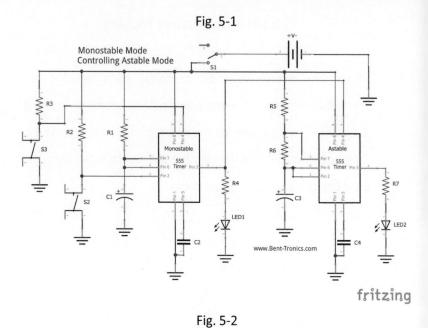

Monostable Mode
Controlling Astable Mode
+V-
S1
R3
R2
R1
S3
S2
C1
Monostable
555
Timer
Pin 8
Pin 4
Pin 7
Pin 6
Pin 2
Pin 3
Pin 1
Pin 5
C2
R4
LED1
R5
R6
C3
Astable
555
Timer
C4
R7
LED2
www.Bent-Tronics.com
fritzing

Fig. 5-2

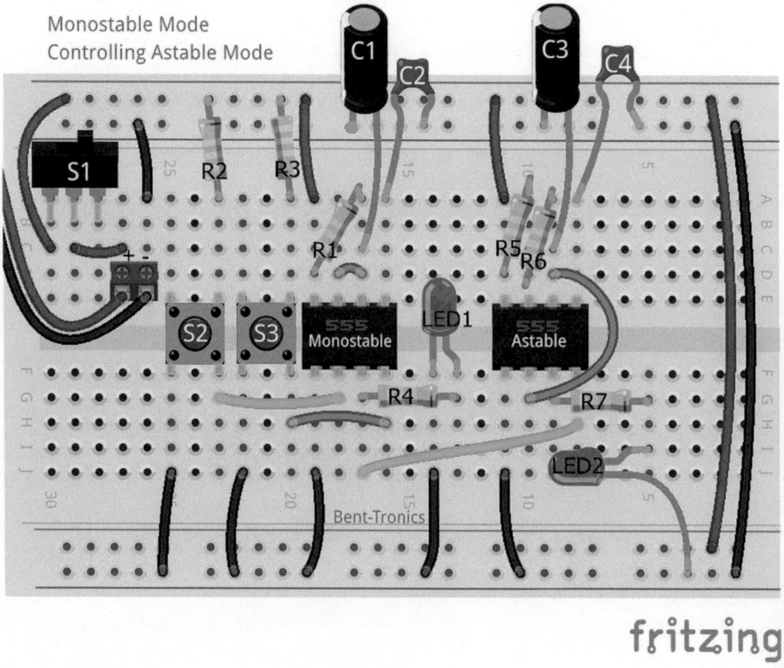

Monostable Mode
Controlling Astable Mode
C1
C2
C3
C4
S1
R2
R3
R1
R5
R6
S2
S3
555
Monostable
LED1
555
Astable
R4
R7
LED2
Bent-Tronics
fritzing

Project 3: Timed Blinker/Buzzer

Parts List:

- Breadboard
- DC Power Supply (a 9-volt battery with some snap-on lead wires attached will do)
- Screw terminal block (one of many methods to hook your battery lead wires to the breadboard)
- Assortment of #22 AWG solid-core hook-up wires
- Two 555 timers
- S1 = Small SPDT slide switch
- S2, S3 = Small SPST push button tactile switch
- **R1 = 1M Ohm*** (Brown, Black, Green)
- R2, R3 = 10k Ohm (Brown, Black, Orange)(pull-up resistors)
- R4, R7 = 470 Ohm (Yellow, Violet, Brown)(or equivalent current limiting resistor for the LED)
- **R5 = 1k Ohm*** (Brown, Black, Red)
- **R6 = 47k Ohm*** (Yellow, Violet, Orange)
- **C1 = 4.7 µF***
- C2, C4 = .01 µF (optional, but recommended)
- **C3 = 1 µF***
- LED1, LED2 = any common LED should work

- additional components for variations of this project as described below: a small speaker

experimenting with these values will change the timing of the 555s - always switch the power off to the circuit before changing parts

   Connect all of the parts except the battery on the breadboard as shown in Fig. 5-2.

Some helpful tips:

- Your parts may look different, or physically be a different size than Fig. 5-2, which may mean a slightly different layout on your breadboard.

- Be sure to observe the polarity markings on your parts. Make sure all anodes (positive) go towards the most positive side of the circuit, and all cathodes (negative) towards the most negative (ground) side of the circuit.

- If any parts seem like they won't fit, leave them off the breadboard and connect them with extra pieces of hook-up wire, which may require soldering.

- Double check, even triple check that all of your connections are correct, and that any wires or legs of any components aren't touching other components or wires.

Once you are confident that your connections are correct, make sure S1 is in its "off" position, then connect the battery, making sure to observe the polarity is correct. Slide S1 to the "on" position, and press S2. What do you see?

If everything is correct, you should see LED1 turn on, LED2 should be blinking at about 15 Hz, and then both turn off after about 5 seconds. Also, pressing S3 after S2 but before 5 seconds is up, should turn off both LEDs. If so, congratulations! If not, switch S1 to the "off" position, disconnect the battery and re-check that all of your connections are correct and that the parts are the right values. Then try again.

Project 3a:

Switch off S1. Change out LED2 for a small speaker. (R7 is optional. The only main difference is the volume. A 10 µF capacitor in series before the speaker to block any DC is recommended for anything more than experimenting.) Switch on S1, then press S2. Do you hear anything? What should you hear? (What was LED2 doing before?) It should be a very low tone (15 Hz will sound more like a clicking noise) while LED1 is on and silence once LED1 turns off.

Feel free to experiment with different timing components for the two 555s as you did in the previous chapters. The monostable equation and timing chart in Fig. 4-5 along with the astable equations and timing chart in Fig. 3-4 can be used to calculate the timing period and frequency for this project. Also, there are many 555 timer calculators available for free on the internet.

Chapter 6: More Mode Mixing

In Chapter 5, you had a monostable 555 controlling an astable 555. By switching roles of the 555s, you can build a rudimentary frequency divider. *Tip: this circuit is only a few steps away from becoming the "Stepped-Tone Generator," a.k.a. Atari Punk Console in Chapter 7!*

Technically speaking, the circuitry for the frequency divider only uses one 555 in monostable mode. However, the easiest way to demonstrate its frequency dividing capability is by having a 555 in astable mode providing the frequency to be divided.

The schematic in Fig. 6-1 looks almost as if you swapped the position of the monostable and astable circuitry in Fig. 5-1. That is very close to what the Fig. 6-1 schematic shows, but not quite. In this circuit, the astable 555's output is triggering pin 2 of the monostable 555, rather than enabling/disabling the reset pin as in Fig. 5-1.

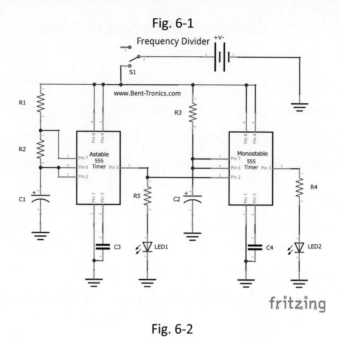

Fig. 6-1

Frequency Divider
+V-
S1
www.Bent-Tronics.com
R1
R2
R3
R4
R5
C1
C2
C3
C4
Astable
555
Timer
Monostable
555
Timer
Pin 8
Pin 4
Pin 7
Pin 6
Pin 2
Pin 3
Pin 1
Pin 5
LED1
LED2
fritzing

Fig. 6-2

Frequency Divider
C1
C3
C2
C4
S1
R1
R2
R3
LED1
LED2
555
Astable
555
Monostable
Bent-Tronics
R5
R4
fritzing

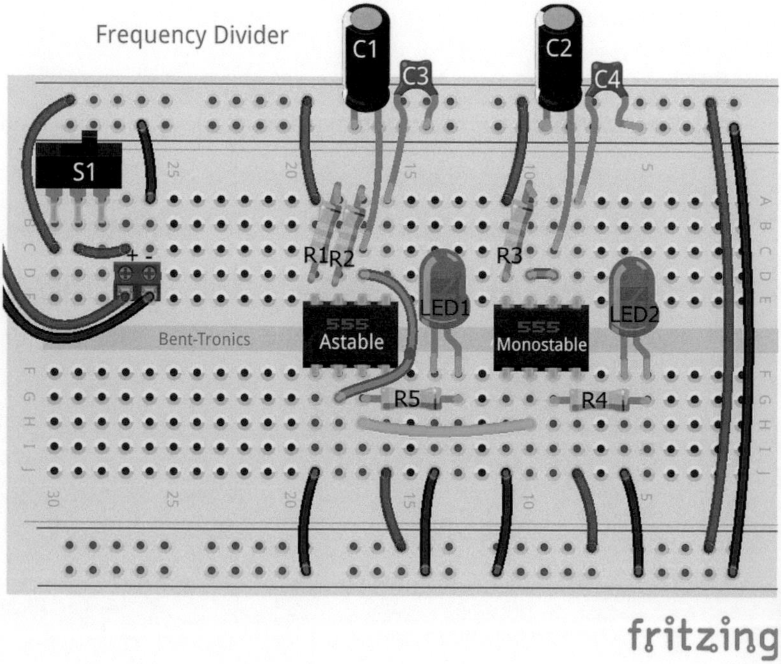

Project 4: Frequency Divider

Parts List:

- Breadboard
- DC Power Supply (a 9-volt battery with some snap-on lead wires attached will do)
- Screw terminal block (one of many methods to hook your battery lead wires to the breadboard)
- Assortment of #22 AWG solid-core hook-up wires
- Two 555 timers
- S1 = Small SPDT slide switch
- **R1 = 1k Ohm*** (Brown, Black, Red)
- **R2 = 47k Ohm*** (Yellow, Violet, Orange)
- **R3 = 47k Ohm*** (Yellow, Violet, Orange)
- R4, R5 = 470 Ohm (Yellow, Violet, Brown)(or equivalent current limiting resistor for the LED)
- **C1 = 1 μF***
- **C2 = 4.7 μF***
- C3, C4 = .01 μF (optional, but recommended)
- LED1, LED2 = any common LED should work

- additional components for variations of this project as described below: one 47k resistor, one .01 μF capacitor, and a small speaker

experimenting with these values will change the timing of the 555s - always switch the power off to the circuit before changing parts

Connect all of the parts except the battery on the breadboard as shown in Fig. 6-2.

Some helpful tips:

- Your parts may look different, or physically be a different size than Fig. 6-2, which may mean a slightly different layout on your breadboard.
- Be sure to observe the polarity markings on your parts. Make sure all anodes (positive) go towards the most positive side of the circuit, and all cathodes (negative) towards the most negative (ground) side of the circuit.
- If any parts seem like they won't fit, leave them off the breadboard and connect them with extra pieces of hook-up wire, which may require soldering.
- Double check, even triple check that all of your connections are correct, and that any wires or legs of any components aren't touching other components or wires.

Once you are confident that your connections are correct, make sure S1 is in its "off" position, then connect the battery, making sure to observe the polarity is correct. Slide S1 to the "on" position. What do you see?

If everything is correct, you should see LED1 blinking at about 15 Hz, and LED2 blinking at a slower rate (1/5th or about 3 Hz). If so, congratulations, you've just built a divide-by-five frequency divider! If not, switch S1 to the "off" position, disconnect the battery and re-check that all of your connections are correct and that the parts are the right values. Then try again.

•Here is a brief and simplified explanation of how this circuit works. The astable (Chapter 3), and monostable (Chapter 4) 555s work as described in their respective sections. The principal concept to understand in this project is the output (pin 3) of the astable 555 is triggering pin 2 of the monostable 555. The monostable 555 ignores additional triggers from the astable 555 (in this example the next four trigger pulses) while it's (the monostable 555) timing cycle is active. Once the timing cycle of the monostable 555 is complete, it can then be triggered again by the astable 555. This cycle repeats indefinitely. The timing period of the monostable 555 needs to be longer than the period of the astable 555 for this circuit to work properly.•

Fig. 6-3 shows that with the selected timing components, for every five output pulses of the astable 555 (aOUT), the monostable 555 produces only one output pulse (mOUT). Also take notice this output pulse from the monostable 555 is the opposite polarity of the output pulses from the astable 555.

Fig. 6-3

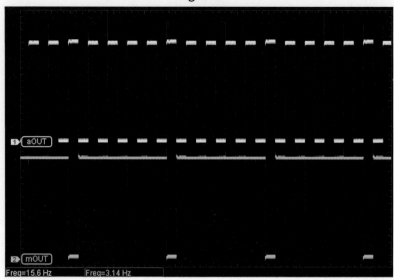

Project 4a:

Switch off S1. Remove LED1 and R5. Replace LED2 with a small speaker. (R4 is optional. The only main difference is the volume. A 10 µF capacitor in series before the speaker to block any DC is recommended for anything more than experimenting.) Change out R1 to a 47k resistor, C1 to a .01 µF capacitor. The astable 555 will now run at a theoretical frequency of 1023 Hz, or a period of .977 milliseconds. To divide that frequency by two, the monostable 555 must have a timing period longer than .977 milliseconds. Change out R3 to a 1k resistor and C2 to a 1 µF capacitor. The monostable 555's theoretical timing period is now 1 millisecond. Switch on S1. You should now hear a tone just over 500 Hz. *Tip: tolerances of the timing components may cause unwanted results, you may need to try different parts and different values to achieve your desired results. A frequency counter or oscilloscope may help with this process.*

The monostable equation and timing chart in Fig. 4-5 along with the astable equations and timing chart in Fig. 3-4 can be used to calculate the timing period and frequency for the proper division ratios for this project. Also, there are many 555 timer calculators available for free on the internet. Feel free to experiment with different values of the timing components. Remember, the timing period of the monostable 555 needs to be longer than the period of the astable 555 for this circuit to work properly.

Chapter 7: Audible Anarchy

Many authors have published noise making circuits that feature the 555. Some of the most popular ones are by Forrest M. Mims III, like his "Stepped-Tone Generator," (Engineer's Mini-Notebook: 555 Circuits; 1984) first described as a "Sound Synthesizer" (Engineer's Notebook: Integrated Circuit Applications, 1980). Later, Kaustic Machines (tiny.cc/KausticAPC) came up with the moniker Atari Punk Console (APC) for this circuit, due to the lo-fi tones it produces. It has been recreated and reimagined in dozens, if not hundreds, of forms. From small DIY kits to full blown synthesizers, the APC circuit has almost taken on a life of its own.

All of the previous projects in this book have led up to understanding the building blocks of the APC. The APC circuit in Fig. 7-1 is almost the same circuit originally published by Mr. Mims. However, this version uses two 555 ICs for clarity, rather than the 556 dual timer in his version.

Fig. 7-1

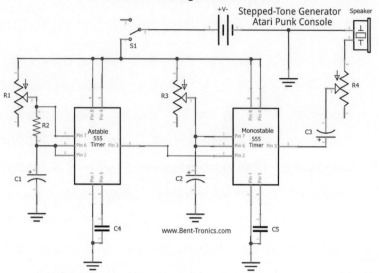

Fig. 7-2

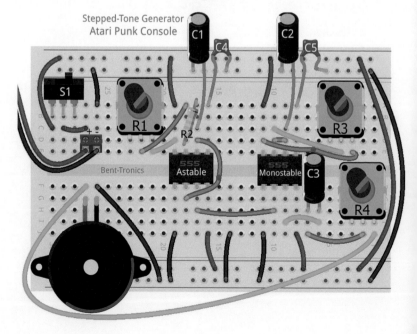

Project 5: "Stepped-Tone Generator" or Atari Punk Console

Parts List:

- Breadboard
- DC Power Supply (a 9-volt battery with some snap-on lead wires attached will do)
- Screw terminal block (one of many methods to hook your battery lead wires to the breadboard)
- Assortment of #22 AWG solid-core hook-up wires
- Two 555 timers
- S1 = Small SPDT slide switch
- **R1, R3 = 500k Ohm Potentiometer***
- **R2 = 1k Ohm*** (Brown, Black, Red)
- R4 = 5k Ohm Potentiometer (optional for volume control)
- **C1 = .01 μF***
- **C2 = .1 μF***
- C3 = 10 μF (it's good practice to put a capacitor in series with a speaker to block any DC)
- a small speaker (8 Ohms preferably)

- additional components for variations of this project as described below: two 1M Ohm Potentiometers

experimenting with these values will change the timing of the 555s - always switch the power off to the circuit before changing parts

Connect all of the parts except the battery on the breadboard as shown in Fig. 7-2. It will be a tight fit!

Some helpful tips:

- Your parts may look different, or physically be a different size than Fig. 7-2, which may mean a slightly different layout on your breadboard.
- Be sure to observe the polarity markings on your parts. Make sure all anodes (positive) go towards the most positive side of the circuit, and all cathodes (negative) towards the most negative (ground) side of the circuit.
- If any parts seem like they won't fit, leave them off the breadboard and connect them with extra pieces of hook-up wire, which may require soldering.
- Double check, even triple check that all of your connections are correct, and that any wires or legs of any components aren't touching other components or wires.

Once you are confident that your connections are correct, make sure S1 is in its "off" position, then connect the battery, making sure to observe the polarity is correct. Slide S1 to the "on" position. What do you hear?

If you don't hear anything, first try turning any or all of the potentiometers (R4 is a volume control). If you still don't hear anything, switch S1 to the "off" position, disconnect the battery and re-check that all of your connections are correct and that the parts are the right values. Then try again.

If you do hear a tone and it changes when adjusting both R1 and R3, congratulations, you've just built the Atari Punk Console! No doubt you will spend the next few minutes (or more) exploring the strange buzzes and tones the APC can produce.

•Here is a brief and simplified explanation of how this circuit works. The astable (Chapter 3), and monostable (Chapter 4) 555s work as described in their respective sections. This project is very similar to the Frequency Divider in Project 4. Where the APC differs is R1 and R3 are adjustable and cause the two 555s to interact with each other "live" versus a static frequency divider. R1 adjusts a "master" frequency of the astable 555, which controls the audible frequency of the monostable 555. R3 changes the frequency dividing ratio and pulse width (resulting in Pulse Width Modulation, or PWM) of the monostable 555. Adjusting R1 and R3 causes audible "steps" in frequency and PWM.•

Project 5a

Mr. Mims has a slightly different version of his classic circuit on the Jameco website, with 1M Ohm potentiometers instead of the 500k ones used above, found here: tiny.cc/APCv2. Switch off S1. Replace the 500k Ohm potentiometers with 1M ones. Switch on S1. Do you notice a difference?

Further experimentation with this circuit is almost limitless. An internet search will reveal countless versions, many replacing the timing potentiometers with CdS cells (a.k.a. photoresistors or LDRs), various resistive touch sensors, etc. Also selectable capacitor values along with various switches for controlling any and all of the above.

Submit pictures or videos of your build at Bent-Tronics.com, on Twitter @BentTronics, or facebook.com/BentTronics to be featured for all to see!

Chapter 8: Bonus Mode

While astable and monostable are the two "standard" operating modes, you can configure the 555 to operate in other "nonstandard" modes. Bistable mode is one of those and the schematic in Fig. 8-1 shows one version.

•Here is a brief and simplified explanation of how this circuit works. Pressing S2 triggers pin 2 LOW, pin 3 goes HIGH, which turns on the LED. Pressing S3 resets pin 4 and pin 3 to LOW, which turns off the LED. That is similar to monostable mode in Fig. 4-2, except that there aren't any timing components in this project, so the on and off state is more of a latching mode, or "Flip-Flop."•

Fig. 8-1:

555 Bistable Mode

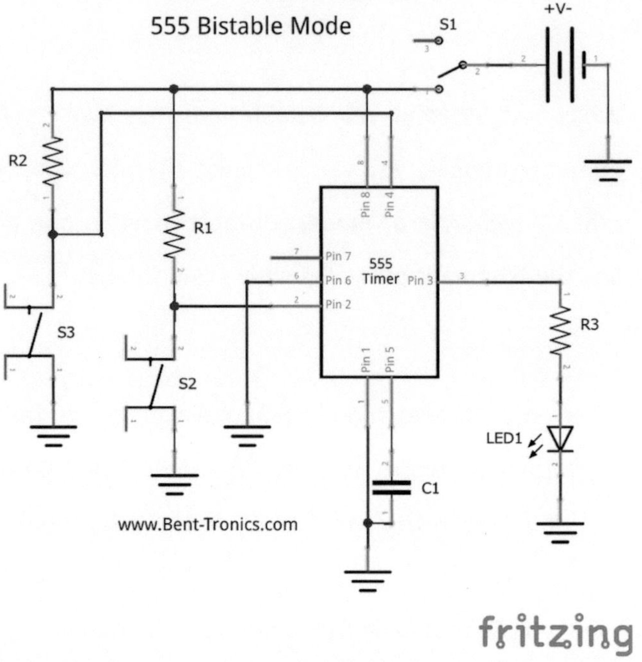

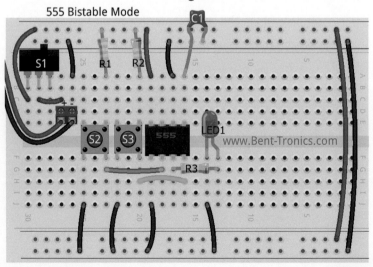

www.Bent-Tronics.com

fritzing

Fig. 8-2

555 Bistable Mode

fritzing

Project 6: Bistable Flip-Flop

Parts List:

- Breadboard
- DC Power Supply (a 9-volt battery with some snap-on lead wires attached will do)
- Screw terminal block (one of many methods to hook your battery lead wires to the breadboard)
- Assortment of #22 AWG solid-core hook-up wires
- 555 timer
- S1 = Small SPDT slide switch
- S2, S3 = Small SPST push button tactile switch
- R1, R2 = 10k Ohm (Brown, Black, Orange)(pull-up resistors)
- R3 = 470 Ohm (Yellow, Violet, Brown)(or equivalent current limiting resistor for the LED)
- C1 = .01 µF (optional, but recommended)

- additional components for variations of this project as described below: an additional LED (LED2), R4 = 470 Ohm (or equivalent current limiting resistor for LED2)

Connect all of the parts except the battery on the breadboard as shown in Fig. 8-2.

Some helpful tips:

- Your parts may look different, or physically be a different size than Fig. 8-2, which may mean a slightly different layout on your breadboard.
- Be sure to observe the polarity markings on your parts. Make sure all anodes (positive) go towards the most positive side of the circuit, and all cathodes (negative) towards the most negative (ground) side of the circuit.
- If any parts seem like they won't fit, leave them off the breadboard and connect them with extra pieces of hook-up wire, which may require soldering.
- Double check, even triple check that all of your connections are correct, and that any wires or legs of any components aren't touching other components or wires.

Once you are confident that your connections are correct, make sure S1 is in its "off" position, then connect the battery, making sure to observe the polarity is correct. Slide S1 to the "on" position. The LED should be off, a short press of S2 should turn the LED on, and it should remain on until a short press of S3 turns off the LED. If not, switch S1 to the "off" position, disconnect the battery and re-check that all of your connections are correct and that the parts are the right values. Then try again.

Project 6a: Sinking and Sourcing

Chapter 2 described the 555's pin functions. The description of pin 3 mentions being able to source and sink up to 200 mA of current (depending on the model of 555). What does this mean? A simplified way to think about current sourcing is that when pin 3 is HIGH, the 555 is the "source" of the current that flows from pin 3, through whatever load (like an LED), then to ground. Current sinking is the opposite. When pin 3 is LOW, current can flow from the positive rail, through a load (like an LED), and "sink" back into pin 3.

The schematic in Fig. 8-3 shows an example of a circuit that can both source and sink current.

Switch S1 to the "off" position, disconnect the battery and add LED2 and R4 as shown in Fig. 8-4.

Fig. 8-3

555 Bistable Mode Sourcing/Sinking

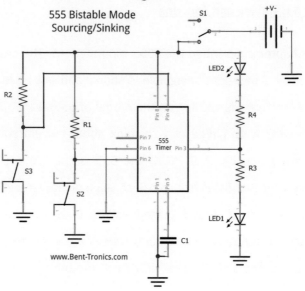

www.Bent-Tronics.com

fritzing

Fig. 8-4

555 Bistable Mode, Sourcing/Sinking

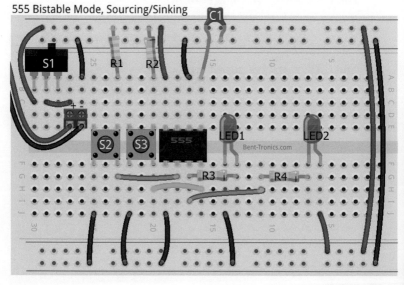

fritzing

58

Once you are confident that your connections are correct, make sure S1 is in its "off" position, then connect the battery, making sure to observe the polarity is correct. Slide S1 to the "on" position. This time you should see LED2 on, then a short press of S2 should turn off LED2 and turn on LED1. A quick press of S3 should switch off LED1 and switch on LED2. When LED1 is on, pin 3 of the 555 is sourcing current. When LED2 is on, pin 3 is sinking current.

If needed, you can apply this sourcing/sinking principle to almost all 555 projects and circuits.

Appendix

References

References used for this book

- Berlin, Howard M. *The 555 Timer Applications Sourcebook With Experiments.* Sams, 1985.
- Gilder, Jules H. *110 IC Timer Projects.* Hayden, 1979.
- Horn, Delton T. *101 Solderless Breadboard Projects.* TAB, 1988.
- Jung, Walter G. *IC Timer Cookbook.* 2nd ed., Sams, 1988.
- Lancaster, Don. *CMOS Cookbook.* 2nd ed., Newnes, 1997.
- Mims III, Forrest M. *Timer, Op Amp & Optoelectronic Circuits & Projects.* Master, 2004.
- Mims III, Forrest M. *Forrest Mims Engineer's Notebook.* 4th ed., Newnes, 1992. (Kindle Version)
- Parr, E.A. *IC 555 Projects.* 4th ed., Babani, 1978.

Online Calculators

- ohmslawcalculator.com/555-astable-calculator
- ohmslawcalculator.com/555-monostable-calculator
- ohmslawcalculator.com/led-resistor-calculator
- ohmslawcalculator.com/ohms-law-calculator
- ohmslawcalculator.com/resistor-colour-chart

Parts List

Complete parts kit for all projects in this book:

- Jameco.com (#2244666) tiny.cc/555kit

Additional Resistor and Capacitor kits from Amazon.com:

- 365 Piece Resistor Kit   tiny.cc/ResistorKit

- 100 Piece Capacitor Kit   tiny.cc/CapacitorKit

Errata and Updates

Please send corrections and suggestions to:
jr@bent-tronics.com.

Bent-Tronics.com will list errata.

Printed in France by Amazon
Brétigny-sur-Orge, FR

16005847R00040